GREEK SACRED SITES

OLYMPIA
THE OLYMPIC GAMES

JILL DUDLEY

PUT IT IN YOUR POCKET SERIES
ORPINGTON PUBLISHERS

Published by
Orpington Publishers

Cover design and origination by
Creeds, Bridport, Dorset
01308 423411

Printed and bound in the UK by
Creeds

© Jill Dudley 2016

ISBN: 978-0-9935378-4-4

OLYMPIA
THE OLYMPIC GAMES

The Olympic Games were part of a great religious festival in honour of Zeus, supreme god of the ancient world. There are several legends regarding the origins of the Olympic Games. Some believe they started very much earlier than the first official Olympiad which was held 776 B.C. It has been suggested they were founded first by Heracles (the Roman name for him was Hercules). He was noted for his strength, endurance and courage and, as the son of Zeus, he may have started them to honour his father.

Another legend was that the site had been chosen by Zeus himself who wanted to be honoured with a festival which would show off the physical strength and abilities of the young men of Greece. Zeus hurled a thunderbolt from his throne on Mt. Olympus and, where it landed, became the site for the Games. It was then named Olympia after Mt. Olympus.

A third legend concerned a man named Pelops. When still an infant Pelops, so it is said, was killed by his father Tantalus who served up the child's shoulder in a dish to the gods; he wanted to see if they could detect the difference between human and animal flesh. They all could, of course, except for Demeter, goddess of corn, who was at the time in a state of deep depression due to the abduction of her young daughter Persephone. In anger at this deception, the gods condemned Tantalas for eternity to Hades, where he was left to stand up to his neck in water which receded every time he leaned forward to assuage his thirst, and branches of fruit hanging which swung out of his reach whenever he tried to grab hold of them to appease his hunger. The gods, however, restored Pelops to life, and replaced his shoulder with an ivory one.

When Pelops grew to manhood, he heard that the local king was offering his daughter as bride to any man able to out-distance him in a chariot race. Whoever failed was killed, and his head mounted on the palace walls. Already twelve suitors had suffered this fate. Pelops presented himself at court but, having no intention of losing his head, he used it instead with cunning. He learned that the king's charioteer was in love with Hippodameia (the king's daughter), and so promised him a night with her if he saw to it that the wheels of the king's chariot fell off during the race. This the charioteer fixed but, when Pelops won the race and, therefore, his bride, he failed to fulfil his side of the bargain, and murdered both the king and the charioteer. It is possible he started the Olympic Games to atone for his deceit and act of treachery.

In the sixth century A.D. two huge earthquakes ravaged the area and the site lay dormant under layers of silt washed down by the two nearby rivers, the Alpheus and the Kladeos. It was not till the nineteenth century that painstaking excavations finally brought the ruins to light.

In ancient times the river Alpheus had been navigable,

and part of the Olympic spectacle was the state barges bringing the dignitaries to the Games. Spectators sailed in by sea from Piraeus, or from outlying colonies, or else came overland down the Peloponnese.

Before every Olympiad a sacred truce was called during which time no one was allowed to take up arms, or to continue legal disputes; thus everyone attending the Games was guaranteed a safe passage. Initially the sacred truce was for one month, but in time it was extended to three months.

Today the archaeological site at Olympia is a conglomeration of carefully identified ruins covering a wide area. To the south are the foundations of the *Prytaneion*, the administration centre, where the holy fire burned continuously on the Sacred Hearth of Hestia, goddess of hearth and home. It was from this flame at Olympia that all sacrificial fires were lit throughout the land on the altars of the gods, and it was even taken for the founding of new colonies.

Nearby was the *Bouleuterion*, an important building to which the athletes would come to swear before a statue of Zeus that they would not cheat, but would observe all the rules of the Games. Beyond the *Bouleuterion* was the Southern Colonnade, once a columned walkway where, at the height of its fame, all who had something to say would try to get themselves heard. It was a public platform for rhetoricians, poets and writers, a market-place for merchants and artisans. It was also a showground for the rich to parade themselves, and for politicians to practise their oratory, knowing that their ideas would spread throughout all Hellas.

To the east of the great Olympic venue in what was

known as the *Altis* (the Sacred Grove in which the temples and altars were), was the great temple of Zeus. All that remains of it now are massive paving slabs and impressively large column drums. It was here in the inner sanctum of the temple, and facing east towards the rising sun, that the majestic cult figure of Zeus seated on a throne was housed; it was said to be one of the seven wonders of the world, created by the sculptor Phidias. It was Phidias who had been responsible for the Parthenon marbles, and the famous cult statue of Athena there.

At Olympia, Phidias had his own workshop and, for the creation of his cult statue of Zeus (which was thirteen metres high), he used ivory, ebony and gold. In his right hand Zeus held a Nike (a winged figure representing victory), and in his left a sceptre topped by an eagle. Interestingly, Phidias had given the face of the god an expression of benevolence and love, instead of the usual features of a powerful, vengeful deity. As one commentator said, a man might wonder about all the other wonders of the world, but this one (the cult statue of Zeus) surpassed them all, causing the viewer to want to kneel in reverence.

It was to this temple, and before this cult statue of the supreme god that, on the last days of the Games, a grand procession came consisting of the judges, administrators, priests and those who had won their event. The winner of each contest would wear a filet of wool around his head and carried a palm branch in his right hand. He stood before the cult statue of the great god and, when the winner's name was called out by the herald, he was crowned with a wreath of wild olive (unlike those who won at the Pythian Games at Delphi who were crowned with a laurel wreath). The occasion was a sort of communion with the god, an acknowledgement that without the god's divine favour and patronage there would have been no victory.

The temple of Zeus itself was tiled with marble roof-tiles, and on the east pediment were sculptures depicting the story of Pelops colluding with the charioteer. Before the temple there had been a great altar, believed to have been where the thunderbolt thrown by Zeus from Mt. Olympus had struck the ground. The altar is thought to have existed as early as the tenth century B.C., and originally had been only a small one; but in time it became an important landmark with a perimeter base of a hundred and twenty-five feet. It had ramps which gave access to a platform up which the sacrifical cattle were driven. The reason for its growth was because the ash from previous sacrifices was never removed. When it reached the height of twenty-two feet, it had steps cut into the compressed and hardened ash-mound so that the priests could have access to the top.

The great sacrifice took place on the third day of the Games, when a solemn procession came from the *Prytaneion* and a hundred bullocks were slaughtered. This took place on the platform below the ash-mound where the carcasses were cut up and the legs carried up the steps to the top where they were burned in honour of Zeus The rest of the meat was used for the Ritual Banquet which was held in the *Prytaneion* on the last evening of the Games. It was believed that Zeus was present at the banquet, and it was a communion between men and deity.

To the north of the temple of Zeus was the *Heraion*,

the temple of Hera, goddess of women and marriage, and wife and sister of Zeus. It was smaller than Zeus' temple and dated to the seventh century B.C., two hundred years earlier than his; till his was built Zeus shared his wife's small temple. Legend has it that Hippodameia, the ill-gotten bride of Pelops, had built the *Heraion* in gratitude to Hera, since she was goddess of marriage. From this marriage their son Atrius was born who became king of Mycenae, and it was his son, Agamemnon*, who commanded the Greek army in the Trojan War.

Further north from the temple of Hera, but still on the east side of the venue was the Stadium. This was constructed around 350 B.C. outside the *Altis* (Sacred Grove). One of the myths regarding its six hundred feet length was that Hercules had run the distance in one breath.

To one side of the Stadium was the Judges' Stand which can still be seen today. Behind it is a gently sloping man-made embankment where as many as forty-five thousand spectators were able to watch the events.

Opposite the Judges' Stand is a small marble altar, still extant, of Demeter Chamyne. There the priestess of Demeter sat enthroned; she was the only woman allowed to watch the races; a strict rule existed forbidding married women to come to the Olympic Games on penalty of death. The priestess of Demeter was the only exception; she had to be married and was chosen from a noble family for each Olympiad. Maybe the goddess was honoured here because she had been the only deity who had been cruelly tricked into eating human flesh served up to the gods by Tantalus.

From there, standing like a row of miniature temples, were

the Treasury Houses, where money and gifts were deposited by the competing city-states or Greek colonies. Each served as a club-house, a convenient meeting place for those who had come from afar. From there it was also possible to watch the races.

To the left of the Stadium there had once been a vaulted tunnel from which the judges and athletes entered the Stadium. It had a bronze trellis-gate which was opened at the beginning of the races allowing only those who were eligible to enter. A part of this tunnel can still be seen.

The events for the five days of the Olympics were as follows: On the first, after the initial swearing-in ceremony in the *Bouleuterior*, there were boys' races, wrestling and boxing contests. On the second, chariot and horse races in the morning, and in the afternoon the pentathlon consisting of throwing the discus, the javelin, jumping, running and wrestling. On day three, after the morning procession of judges, ambassadors and competitors, and after the official sacrifice of the hundred oxen at the great Altar of Zeus in the morning, there followed foot-races. Day four consisted of wrestling, boxing and the penkatrion which was a fight to get the opponent to the ground and never mind the means. This was followed in the afternoon by a race in full armour. On day five was the final procession to the temple of Zeus and the crowning of the victors.

The Olympic Games continued to flourish until the Christian era. Regarding the Games as a pagan abomination, the Emperor Theodosius I closed down the site, in fact closed down all pagan temples. Theodosius II went further and decreed their complete destruction, and so it was that the temples at Olympia were destroyed.

In the nineteenth century there was an upsurge of interest in the Greek classical period, and in 1829 a French team of archaeologists began excavations around the temple of Zeus. In 1896 the old Olympic Games were revived, and were held in Athens since it was in Greece that the Games originated. Today, at the modern Torch Lighting ceremony, the Olympic flame is lit by the sun at the ancient site of Olympia before being relayed around the globe to end up in the country hosting the Games. The only thing that is missing from the modern Games and should surely be renewed, is the calling of a Sacred Truce during which period all countries lay down their arms, and in the few months of global peace, people travel to the Games in safety.

* Denotes a separate booklet on the subject.

FAMILY TREE OF THE GODS AND GODDESSES

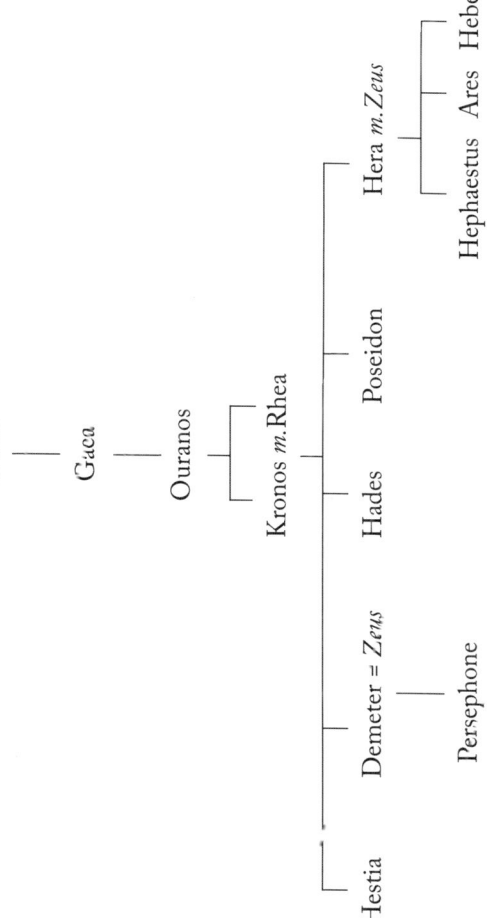

GLOSSARY OF GODS AND GODDESSES

ATHENA – Goddess of victory, weaving and handicraft, and also protectress of many cities, but especially Athens. She was the embodiment of wisdom, and in the classical era her symbol was the owl.

DEMETER – Goddess of corn and agriculture, and mother of Persephone, otherwise known as Kore.

HADES – Brother of Zeus, and god of the underworld.

HERA – Wife and sister of Zeus. She was goddess of women and marriage.

HESTIA – Goddess of the hearth, symbol of the home and family. She was the daughter of Kronos and Rhea.

KORE – (See Persephone).

KRONOS – A Titan. He was married to Rhea who gave birth to many of the Olympian gods. His name means 'time'.

PERSEPHONE – Daughter of Demeter. She was abducted by Hades and became queen of the underworld.

RHEA – A Titaness. She was wife of Kronos, and mother of Hestia, Hera and Zeus, and several other Olympian gods.

TITANS – The offspring of Ouranos (often spelt Uranus, the heavens) and Gaea (the earth). There were said to be twelve of them, six sons and six daughters. Kronos was one of the sons, and Rhea one of the daughters. These two gave birth to Hestia, Hera and Zeus and some other Olympian gods.

ZEUS – Son of Kronos and Rhea. He was supreme god of the ancient world having deposed his father. He was god of the heavens, the giver of law, and the disperser of justice.

MORE FROM THE
PUT IT IN YOUR POCKET SERIES
GREEK MYTHS

TROJAN WAR
THE JUDGEMENT OF PARIS
HELEN
KING AGAMEMNON
ACHILLES
THE WOODEN HORSE
ODYSSEUS

ISLANDS
CHIOS – HOMER
CRETE – THESEUS AND THE MINOTAUR
KOS – HIPPOCRATES AND ASCLEPIUS
NAXOS – THESEUS AND ARIADNE
RHODES – THE COLOSSUS
SANTORINI – THE LOST ISLAND OF ATLANTIS

ALSO BY JILL DUDLEY

YE GODS! (TRAVELS IN GREECE)

YE GODS! II (MORE TRAVELS IN GREECE)

LAP OF THE GODS (TRAVELS IN CRETE
AND THE AEGEAN ISLANDS)